Calvinism
and the Declaration
of Independence

Thomas Adamo

A Woodbine Cottage Publication

A Woodbine Cottage Publication
PO Box 211
Lakehurst, NJ 08733-0211
awcpublications@aol.com

Copyright 2010

ISBN: 1-4536-9012-3
EAN-13: 978-1-4536-9012-3

Thomas Adamo is a professor of speech and rhetoric. His
areas of study and research include communication theory,
political philosophy, history, and media studies.

Calvinism
and the Declaration
of Independence

Thomas Adamo

INTRODUCTION

The American War of Independence was one of the first political upheavals in history based primarily on ideology. Subsequent history has demonstrated the importance of philosophical justification for the instigation of any radical political action of comparable ambition to the Revolution of 1776. However, in recent years the true nature of the ideas that helped fortify the American revolutionaries has come into question, with much of this controversy centering on the true origin of the concepts contained in the Declaration of Independence and the Constitution. According to one textbook, the ideology which Jefferson propounded in the Declaration of Independence was solely a product of the eighteenth-century Enlightenment.[1] While Jefferson was particularly influenced by the Enlightenment, he wrote the Declaration of Independence on behalf of the entire

---

[1] Wells, p. 124.

Continental Congress, most of whom shared their constituents' more traditional beliefs. In the words of Perry Miller, "Rationalism was never so widespread as liberal historians, or those fascinated by Jefferson, have imagined."[2]

Therefore, the need has arisen to investigate whether the political traditions of the United States were entirely products of the Enlightenment. The greatest contender against the idea of an ideology based solely on the Enlightenment is the Calvinistic-Reformed-Puritan tradition of England and her American colonies. While the Reformed tradition of the Anglo-American culture may not take exclusive credit for the ideological traditions that influenced the Revolution in the colonies, its influence was great. Four case studies of political thought will demonstrate the influence of Calvinistic philosophical traditions on the American Revolution. Some areas of interest will include the role of government in society, natural law, the

---

[2] Schaeffer, vol. 5, p. 490.

idea that government exists by the consent of the governed, references to Providence and the relationship that is to exist between religion and government.

Four individual thinkers will combine to demonstrate the progressive influence of Reformed thinking on the conception of the ideas that fortified the Revolution and the infant Republic. The first study shall be devoted to John Calvin, one of the great Protestant reformers whose influence was monumental in all areas of thought. His thought concerning government will be examined as the foundation upon which subsequent Reformed thought was built using primary and secondary sources with particular focus on his <u>Institutes of the Christian Religion</u> and one of his other significant works <u>A Commentary on Daniel</u>.

The second case study will concern itself with the Rev. Samuel Rutherford, a Scottish minister who was the Rector of St. Andrews University in Scotland and was a delegate to the Westminster Assembly in

1643. Rutherford is noteworthy because his primary political work, <u>Lex Rex</u> or <u>The Law and The King</u>, espoused many of the theories utilized by John Locke, and in turn Thomas Jefferson, yet Rutherford predated both these men and all of the philosophies of the Enlightenment by many years. The importance of Rutherford is crucial due to his intellectual relationship to Locke, which provides a bridge between the Calvinist theology and Locke's more secular philosophy that was directly influential upon the Declaration of Independence. In the study of Rutherford, <u>Lex Rex</u> will be the work of primary of investigation due to the small number of secondary source available concerning it.

John Locke, with particular emphasis on <u>The Second Treatise of Civil Government</u>, will provide a crucial transitional step between the consciously Reformed ideas of Calvin and Rutherford, and the pronouncements of the Declaration of Independence. Although Locke was an important thinker of the early

Enlightenment, he still identified himself strongly with Protestant Christianity.

Finally, various writing of Thomas Jefferson will demonstrate how much of his political ideology, though he might never admit it, was descended from the Reformed-Calvinist tradition. Jefferson was the obvious colonial thinker to put in this place due to his involvement in the writing of the Declaration of Independence and his influence over the early policies of the United States. Moreover, according to Norman De Jong, Jefferson "loathed Calvinists and rejected their belief in a sovereign, providential God who was directly involved in mapping the course of history."[3] Subsequently, by demonstrating the reliance of Jefferson on Calvinism for his political thought (albeit indirectly) this would, in consequence, illustrate the certainty that his fellow Founding Fathers, many of whom possessed an openly Reformed weltanschauung, or philosophy of life, were directly influenced by

---

[3] De Jong, p. 34.

Calvinism in their attempts to secede from England and establish Republican government on the North American continent.

John Calvin

John Calvin and his theology are crucially important when the origins of the political thought that eventually lead to the founding of the United States are considered. Calvin was most famous for his colossal work <u>Institutes of the Christian Religion,</u> which he viewed as an introduction to the study of biblical doctrine. While this tome expounded a theology that was in keeping with the fundamentals of main line Protestantism of the time, "His statements on political theory were less traditional."[4] The nature of some of his unusual statements was such that one early source stated "John Calvin was virtually the founder of America."[5] Some of the areas in which Calvin made several of his strongest arguments included natural law, the separation of church and state, as well as the proper relationship between the government and the people.

---

[4] Dillenberger, p. 20.
[5] McFetridge, p. 68.

Moreover, the doctrine of the Church that Calvin espoused included ideas of constitutionalism, the election of leaders, and the liberty of conscience. These contributions were so immense, John Dillenberger, an eminent historian of the Reformation, has stated, "It is conceivable that the Constitution of the United States ... owes as much to John Calvin as it does to the artificial checks and balances of Montesquieu."[6]

Among some individuals, Calvinism has acquired a bad reputation for a variety of reasons. Nevertheless, within the concerns of civil government, "Calvinism is acknowledged, even by its foes, to have promoted powerfully the cause of civil liberty."[7] A useful document with which to gain a preliminary knowledge of the role of government, as defined by Calvin, is the <u>Genevan Confession of 1536</u>. In the twenty-first article of this work, "Concerning Magistrates," Calvin stated:

---

[6] Dillenberger, p. 20.
[7] Fisher, p. 239.

We hold the supremacy and dominion of kings and princes as also of other magistrates and officers, to be a holy thing and a good ordinance of God. And since in performing their office they serve God and follow a Christian vocation, whether in defending the afflicted and innocent, or in correcting and punishing the malice of the perverse, we on our part also ought to accord them honour and reverence, to render respect and subservience, to execute their commands, to bear the charges they impose on us, so far as we are able without offence to God. In sum, we ought to regard them as vicars and lieutenants of God, whom one cannot resist without resisting God himself; and their office is a sacred commission from God, which has been given them so that they may rule and govern us.[8]

In summary, Calvin viewed the magistracy as an office appointed by God with the role of protecting the innocent and punishing lawbreakers. The magistrate was a political minister of the Lord, deserving all obedience, unless there was a demand made contrary to the law of God.

Proceeding from this foundation, Calvin developed a complex theory of government intricately connected with his theological views. His <u>Institutes of the Christian Religion</u>, completed in 1559, provides the most complete development of Calvin's beliefs concerning government. Early portions of his opus included his investigation of the area which later thinkers would label natural law. In this area, as in others, Calvin began with God as his primary point of reference, stating, "There is within the human mind, and

---

[8] Manschreck, p. 93.

indeed by natural instinct, an awareness of divinity."[9] This was an important tenet, because Calvin clearly acknowledged the use of religion as a form of mind control over the "common folk" at various times. He believed that the instinctive knowledge of God within every human mind explained the ease of such religious subjugation. With this concept of the nature of humanity firmly in mind, Calvin strongly affirmed (perhaps in anticipation of much modern philosophical speculation): "it is utterly vain for some men to say that religion was invented by the subtlety and craft of a few to hold the simple folk in thrall by this device and that those very persons who originated the worship of God for others did not in the least believe that any God existed."[10]

For Calvin, God is the primary cause of all things. Nevertheless, from the human perspective intermediary or secondary causes are often the means of

---

[9] Calvin, <u>Institutes</u>, I.iii.1.
[10] Ibid., I.iii.2.

enacting the will of the Lord on earth. As Calvin put it, if a "godly man suffers any loss because of negligence of imprudence, he will conclude that it came about by the Lord's will, but will also impute it to himself."[11]   Thus, God is sovereign but man is still responsible for his actions. Therefore, it is inexcusable for man to claim ignorance of the "sense of divinity ... by nature engraven on human hearts."[12] Moreover, this "sense of divinity" has concretely practical applications in the real world, for, as Calvin later stated: "natural law is that apprehension of the conscience which distinguishes sufficiently between just and unjust, and which deprives men of the excuse of ignorance, while it proves them guilty by their own testimony."[13] However, recognizing the inability of an intuitive natural law to achieve a practical reality before God, Calvin proceeded to affirm, in his discussion of the Ten Commandments, "the Lord has provided

---

[11] Ibid, I.xvii.9.
[12] Ibid, I.iv.4.
[13] Ibid, II.ii.22.

us with a written law to give us a clear witness of what was too obscure in the natural law."[14]   In affirming this, Calvin demonstrated that there is a binding natural law over all humanity, obscured due to sin but clarified through divine revelation. The important fact is that Calvin's thoughts pertaining to government presupposed the doctrine of natural law, despite the opinions of various commentators to the contrary, such as August Lang who argued that Calvin was not "a friend of natural law."[15]

For Calvin, the Ten Commandments embodied, in a cumulative sense, everything towards which human law strives. This law was further divide into two distinct "Tables" concerning the duties of the individual towards God and towards man. Dividing the content and purpose of law in this way was essential for Calvin who maintained that the Tables were separate and yet interdependent, for "apart from the

---

[14] Ibid, II.viii.1 & 2.
[15] Armstrong, pp. 68-9.

fear of God men do not preserve equity and love among themselves."[16] As he phrased it at another point, "If a man say, I love God, and hateth his brother, he is a liar: for he that loveth not his brother whom he hath seen, how can he love God whom he hath not seen? And this commandment have we from him, That he who loveth God love his brother also."[17] Therefore, the relationship an individual has with God will influence his or her action towards other people. By applying this principle of the division of the Law into two Tables to the government of human society, Calvin later concluded: "there is a twofold government in man: one aspect is spiritual, whereby the conscience is instructed in piety and in reverencing God; the second is political, whereby man is educated for the duties of humanity and citizenship that must be maintained among men."[18]

This division, on the part of Calvin,

---

[16] Calvin, Institutes, II.viii.11.
[17] 1 John 4:20-21. The Bible. King James Version.
[18] Calvin, Institutes, III.xix.15.

between the church and the state was perhaps his most radical break with traditional political theory, despite the fact that he felt each branch, while distinct, should compliment the other.[19]   To summarize the theory of Calvin thus far: he believed in an absolute natural law that was binding upon all humanity.   However, human sin obscured this natural law. Therefore, the Old Testament Law was to testify to the laws of nature.   Within the laws that God had given he perceived a division between spiritual and civil law. Following this separation to its logical conclusion, he argued for a separation between the Church, or the spiritual government, and the State, or the political government, with both governments simultaneously working on complimentary terms with one another.[20]   Only with an understanding of this complex premise can the student of Calvin begin to delve into his writings concerning civil government as

---

[19] Wendel, p. 79.
[20] Calvin, Institutes, IV.xx.1-2.

contained in the final chapter of the final book of the <u>Institutes</u>.

In keeping with his former premises, Calvin viewed the magistracy as ordained by God. Along with its duty to maintain public morality, Calvin believed that government was crucial to society because "it prevents the public peace from being disturbed; it provides that each man may keep his property safe and sound ... In short, it provides that a public manifestation of religion may exist among Christians, and that humanity be maintained among men."[21] Calvin believed any type of government is preferable to anarchy, such as when he commented in <u>Daniel</u>: "tyranny is better than anarchy ... because where there is no supreme governor there is none to preside and keep the rest in check."[22] He viewed the magistrate as the political deputies of God who were responsible to him alone. For Calvin, this did not allow the government

---

[21] Ibid, IV.xv.3.
[22] Calvin, <u>Daniel</u>, IV.10-16.

to sanctify its action through religion; rather political figures were to be zealous to establish a righteous society of justice and mercy, for the glory of God "to whom they must hereafter render account of the administration of their charge."[23]

Calvin maintained that speculating about what form of government would be the best for men was little more than an "idle pastime" for unqualified men with nothing better to do. He felt that the form of government a particular region would choose was largely dependent upon local circumstances. As to his own opinion of the best form of government, Calvin stated:

> I will not deny that aristocracy, or a system compounded of aristocracy and democracy, far excels all others: not indeed of itself, but ... men's fault or failings causes it to be safer and more bearable for a number to exercise government, so that

---

[23] Calvin, <u>Institutes</u>, IV.xx.6.

they may help one another, teach and admonish one another; and if one asserts himself unfairly, there may be a number of censors and masters to restrain his willfulness.[24]

For Calvin, a society that had multiple bases of power was superior, for such a situation would disallow, in most cases, total centrality which contained the greatest possibility of violating the freedom of the people, this liberty being one of the primary goals of government. Nevertheless, Calvin believed compliance and obedience was due to any ruler regardless of the type government.

Calvin upheld the responsibility of the government to be involved with the proclamation of both of the Tables of the Law mentioned above, for "no government can be happily established unless piety is the first concern; and ... those laws are preposterous which neglect God's right and

---

[24] Ibid, IV.xx.8.

provide only for men."[25] Moreover, "kings are bound to defend the worship of God, and to execute vengeance upon those who profanely despise it."[26] Thus, the government was not neutral on moral and religious questions, but rather to support the piety of the population in order to perpetuate a just society. While upholding the right of the government to levy taxes and wage war, Calvin looked towards law, "the stoutest sinews of the commonwealth," to be a "silent magistrate" before which all men would be equal.[27] In addition, the immutability of law was crucial, for "When laws are variable, many are necessarily injured, and no private interest is stable unless the law be without variation; besides, when there is liberty in changing laws, license succeeds in place of justice."[28] Thus, nations are permitted to issue laws that do not contradict the natural law (as revealed in the Decalogue, or the

---

[25] Ibid, IV.xx.9.
[26] Calvin, Daniel, IV.1-3.
[27] Calvin, Institutes, IV.xx.14.
[28] Calvin, Daniel, VI.10.

"perpetual rule of love" as Calvin called it), provided the ultimate goal is equity between individuals.[29]   For this reason, Calvin was ardent in his defense of the judicial system as the institution for the application of the power of law within society.[30]

From this juncture, Calvin began to expound some of his most controversial theories concerning the obedience that is due to any ruler, even an unjust one. He began by expostulating that, as ministers of God, magistrates are due reverence because of the dignity of their office, even if the individual is less than honorable.[31]   This deference must be sincere, according to Calvin, because "the magistrate cannot be resisted without God being resisted at the same time."[32]   Moreover, Calvin realized that not all kings are good kings, nevertheless obedience was to be rendered unto them for "empires are bestowed upon

---

[29] Calvin, Institutes, IV.xx.15 & 16.
[30] Ibid, IV.xx.17-21.
[31] Ibid, IV.xx.22.
[32] Ibid, IV.xx.23.

men by divine power and not by chance ... There is no power but of God."[33] Therefore, Calvin affirmed "a private citizen who lays his hand upon a tyrant is openly condemned by the heavenly judge," left open the question of how wicked kings were to be restrained.[34]   In this type of situation, Calvin stated, "that it is not for us to remedy such evils; that only this remains, to implore the Lord's help, in whose hands are the hearts of kings, and the changing of kingdoms."[35]   This alternative may sound too numinous to be practical unless remembering that while God is the primary cause of all events, on earth he often uses intermediary sources through which to express his will.[36]   In a situation where tyranny has usurped the rightful role of civil government, Calvin advised the following:

　　　If the correction of unbridled

---

[33] Calvin, <u>Daniel</u>, V.18-20. See also: <u>Institutes</u>, IV.xx.24-6.
[34] Calvin, <u>Institutes</u>, III.x.6; IV.xx.28.
[35] Ibid, IV.xx.29.

despotism is the Lord's to avenge, let us not at once think that it is entrusted to us, to whom no command has been given except to obey and suffer. I am speaking all the while of private individuals. For if there are now any magistrates of the people, appointed to restrain the willfulness of kings ... I am so far from forbidding them to withstand, in accordance with their duty, the fierce licentiousness of kings, that, if they wink at kings who violently fall upon and assault the common folk, I declare that their dissimulation involves nefarious perfidy, because they dishonestly betrays the freedom of the people, of which they have been appointed protectors by God's ordinance.[37]

---

[36] See footnote #8.
[37] Calvin, Institutes, IV.xx.31.

Therefore, while Calvin firmly held to the conviction forbidding private citizens from taking the restraint of the civil government into their own hands, he also advanced the idea that lower, local magistrates are responsible to preserve the liberty of the population, the primary purpose of civil government.[38] This principle was of primary importance for Calvin in those situations when the political authority attempted to breach the separation between it and the Church, or the spiritual government: "earthly princes lay aside all their power when they rise up against God, and are unworthy of being reckoned in the number of mankind."[39] "So should we act toward princes, lords and every kind of superior. It is unworthy and absurd for their eminence so to prevail as to pull down the loftiness of God. On the contrary, their eminence depends upon God's loftiness and ought to lead us to

---

[38] See footnote #21
[39] Calvin, <u>Daniel</u>, VI.22.

it."[40] He later stated, "The Lord, therefore, is the King of Kings, who, when he has opened his sacred mouth, must alone be heard, before all and above all men."[41] Thus, Calvin returned to the starting point of his discussion that God, obedience to him and the furtherance of his glory, is the chief purpose for all individual action. In doing so, he ends his discussion on government stating that the zeal for the glory of God should overshadow everything else within the realm of this life.

Finally, Calvin's concepts of local church government had republican implications that would influence subsequent history. In the words of George Fisher, "Men who were accustomed to rule themselves in the Church, would claim the same privilege in the commonwealth."[42] First, Calvin advocated the necessity of church constitutions, because "no organization is sufficiently strong unless constituted with

---

[40] Calvin, <u>Institutes</u>, II.viii.38.
[41] Ibid, IV.xx.32.
[42] Fisher, p. 240.

definite laws."[43]   This was necessary to keep good order within the church, although Calvin was also uncompromising in his insistence that such constitutions be arranged along biblical lines and should be kept by individuals with a free conscience.[44] In citing ancient practices of the church that in the choosing of elders, the "agreement of the citizens was always required."[45]   Thus, according to one commentator,   "Calvinistic   doctrines, asserts that all power is vested in the Church; that is, in the people."[46]   When secularized, these doctrines concerning the Church   bring   forth   concepts   of constitutional law, liberty of conscience and the election of political leaders.

From this brief examination of the political philosophy of Calvin, it is clear that his doctrines were antecedents of more contemporary   political   thought.   This included his conception of natural law,

---

[43] Calvin, <u>Institutes</u>, IV.x.27.
[44] Ibid, IV.x.28, 30 & 31.
[45] Ibid, IV.iv.10.
[46] McFetridge, p. 9.

which he saw as clarified in the Law of the Old Testament. In this Law, he perceived a twofold division between duties towards God and man, leading to his distinction between the spheres of influence for the Church and the State, a radical concept though he intended the two branches to be complimentary. Calvin viewed government as ordained by God for preserving liberty, property and the worship of the Lord. Magistrates were to revere as ministers of God, making rebellion sinful- even against a wicked ruler. However, due to his belief that political power should have more than one focal point, Calvin gave the responsibility of restraining the wickedness of kings to local magistrates. His doctrine of the government of the Church contained many points reminiscent of modern political theory. De Tocqueville has described Calvinism as "a democratic and republican religion," and this fact was crucial in view of it influence on subsequent history, especially in the foundation of the American republic.[47]

Samuel Rutherford

As a Scot, Samuel Rutherford had a rich Protestant heritage in the area of resistance to tyranny that proceeded from John Knox, the first Reformer to develop a theory of justified revolution.[48] In fact, at its time of publication Lex Rex was merely one of dozens of political tracts advocating resistance to tyranny. This particular work became prominent due to its "being exhaustive ... and it contained the principles of revolution upon which all major Protestant parties in England agreed."[49] This work's revolutionary character fomented great controversy within England following the restoration of monarchy. Lex Rex was subversive to the entire social order. Nevertheless, within the area of civil resistance, the thought of Rutherford was hardly new. Like Calvin, "Rutherford stresses the need for representation by a duly appointed official; the Bible does not

---

[48] Schaeffer, Vol.5, p. 472.
[49] Amos, p. 140.

authorize any one ruler to take the law into his own hands."[50] The crucial importance of Rutherford ideas lays in their place a precursor to the work of John Locke. According to Gary Amos, "It can ... be safely supposed that Locke was familiar with Lex Rex. Locke's father was a leading Puritan in Parliament who knew Rutherford.   Locke was a student at Westminster just two years after Lex Rex was published there, causing a great stir."[51]

As a representative of Scotland at the Westminster Assembly of 1643, Rutherford holds impeccable credentials as a Calvinist, especially when one considers the fact that the Westminster Confession is the standard that measures churches of the Reformed tradition, even to the present day. In his thought, as a theologian and as a professor, Rutherford hoped to demonstrate the need for "a government of law rather than of the arbitrary decisions of men-because the Bible as the final authority

---

[50] Whitehead, p. 156.
[51] Amos, p. 216, fn. 79.

was there as the base."[52] The twenty-third section of the Westminster Confession of Faith, which Rutherford assisted in writing, provides some useful insight concerning Puritan views of government:

1. God, the supreme Lord and King of all the world, hath ordained civil magistrates to be under him over the people, for his own glory, and the public good; and, to this end, hath armed them with the power of the sword, for the defense and encouragement of them that are good, and for the punishment of evil-doers.

2. It is lawful for Christians to accept and execute the office of magistrate, when called thereunto, in the managing whereof, as they ought especially to maintain piety, justice and peace, according to the

[52] Schaeffer, Vol. 5, p. 138.

wholesome laws of each commonwealth; so, for that end, they may lawfully, now under the New Testament, wage war upon just and necessary occasions.

3. The civil magistrate may not assume to himself the administration of the word and sacraments, or the power of the keys of the rulerdom of heaven: yet he hath authority, and it is his duty, that unity and peace be preserved in the church, that the truth of God be kept pure and entire, that all blasphemies and heresies be suppressed, all corruptions and abuses in worship and discipline prevented or reformed, and all the ordinances of God duly settled, administered and observed. For the better effecting whereof, he hath power to call synods, to be present at them, and to provide that whatsoever is transacted in

them are according to the mind of God.

4. It is the duty of the people to pray for magistrates, to honor their persons, to pay them tribute and other dues, to obey their lawful commands, and to be subject to their authority for conscience' sake. Infidelity or difference in religion, doth not make void the magistrate's just and legal authority, nor free the people from their due obedience to him: from which ecclesiastical persons are not exempted; much less hath the Pope any power or jurisdiction over them in their dominions or lives, if he shall judge them to be heretics, or upon any other pretence whatsoever.[53]

This statement reveals several important Calvinist principles regarding

---

[53] Williamson, p. 240-4.

civil government. Among these are the beliefs that God has ordained civil government for his glory. In addition, the government holds the "power of the sword" with which to punish evildoers. Unlike Calvin, the Confession does not advocate a separation of the church and civil government. Rather, it gives the magistrate the charge of keeping peace within the church. Finally, Christians are to be obedient to the "lawful commands" of the government, even in cases when the religion of individual and state do not coalesce on all matters. This last point would be important for Rutherford as he formulated his theories of government in <u>Lex Rex</u>, because the actions and reactions of the populace in certain situations resulted from the parameters of what is lawful for a government to command. In <u>Lex Rex</u>, Rutherford primarily expanded upon this short statement.

Part of the reason for the great opposition to <u>Lex Rex</u> was the fact that Rutherford based his arguments primarily on Scripture, a potent force in an age that universally accepted the Bible as the Word of God. Rutherford used a question and answer format throughout his work. His first consideration was to determine the divine authorization for government in the current state of creation. As he observed this fundamental question, Rutherford determined that there are three types of government: monarchy, aristocracy, and democracy (government by one, few, or all). Equating divine law to be synonymous with natural law, Scripture determined that "All civil power is from God in its root," although Rutherford emphasized "We cannot but put difference betwixt the institution of the office, viz. government, and the designation of person or persons to the office."[54] Put another way, all civil authority ultimately derives from the ordinance of God, and of all the various forms of government there is no one that is more sanctified than the others are. Furthermore, Rutherford maintained a

---

[54] Rutherford, Q 1, p. 1.

distinction between a particular office and the occupant of that office. Therefore, the office of governor deserves obedience even if the individual office holder is disliked personally. However, this principle did not give absolute authority to civil government, for Rutherford also stated; "Now God only by a divine law can lay a band of subjection on the conscience."[55] Thus, while individuals may be subject to the authorities in their actions, they are accountable only to God for their thoughts.

From the foundation above, Rutherford proceeded to consider the natural reasons for civil government. The primary presupposition concerning who should govern was that "if all men be born equally free, there is no reason in nature why one man should be ruler and lord over another." Moreover, he would later show the equality of men to be evident through the doctrine of Original Sin.[56] This point was extremely important to Rutherford as

---

[55] Ibid.
[56] Rutherford, Q 2, p. 2; Q 7, p. 25.

he later developed it with regard to liberty, for "Slavery ... is not natural, but against nature ... Man is born by nature free from all subjection ... especially he is free of subjection to a prince by nature."[57] Human freedom posed a dilemma for Rutherford regarding how to justify the existence of any government at all. He resolved this problem by considering government valid through a "secondary law of nature." In other words, "it is lawful to repel violence by violence; and this is a special act of the magistrate."[58] By this, Rutherford established government officials as the medium within society responsible for the maintenance of a just and lawful order between individuals and groups; remembering at this point, he was not advocating a particular form of government, but government in general. Nevertheless, the problem remained of who should receive the authority to govern. Again turning to the Bible, he stated, "the

---

[57] Rutherford, Q 13, p. 51.
[58] Rutherford, Q 2, p. 3.

Scripture's arguments may well be drawn from the school of nature," concluding, "power of government is immediately from God, and this or that definite power is mediately from God, proceeding from God by the mediation of the consent of a community, which resigneth their power to one or more rulers."[59]   Thus, while the power of government ultimately proceeds through the will of God, communal consent is the secondary cause for a specific establishment within a community or nation.

Rutherford, as a Calvinist, believed that God ordains all things.   This concept applied to all areas of life including government: "The ruler may be said to be from God and his word."   The office of ruler was a holy vocation, because:

> The execution of their office is an act of the just Lord of heaven and earth, not only by

---

[59] Rutherford, Q 3, p. 3. (See Jeremiah 43:10, 27:6; Romans 13:1.)

permission, but according to God's revealed will in his word; their judgment is not the judgment of men, but of the Lord ... So, if the ruler be a living law by office, and the law put in execution which God hath commanded, then, as the moral law is by divine institution, so must the officer of God be ... the keeper, preserver, and avenger of God's law.[60]

Again Rutherford spoke of civil government in general, because "they are not governments different in nature ... they differ politically and positively."[61] Thus, whether a specific government is a monarchy, aristocracy, or democracy, they all serve the same purpose before God. In fact, Rutherford considered government, although ordained by God, "an ordinance

---

[60] Rutherford, Q 3, p. 4. (See 1 Chronicles 12:10, 2 Chronicles 19:6.)
[61] Rutherford, Q 3, p. 5.

of men ... because exercised by man."[62]

Describing the concept of civil government as founded by God and practiced by men; Rutherford went on to describe the nature of this ordinance with particular reference to monarchy. Rutherford viewed the power of a monarchy to be derivative from God, while its effectual establishment came from the people. In his own words: "The question is, whether the rulerly office itself comes from God. I conceive it is, and floweth from the people ... God ordained the power. It is from the people only by a virtual emanation, in respect that a community having no government at all may ordain a ruler or appoint an aristocracy."[63] While the point would later be made "To be a ruler is a free gift of God," the crown was given in a tangible sense "by way of free donation" of the people who, having given the power conditionally, were free to rescind this

---

[62] Rutherford, Q 3, p. 6.
[63] Rutherford, Q 4, p. 6. (See 1 Samuel 11:15, 2 Kings 10:5, 1 Chronicles 12:32.)

grant when the condition had been violated by a ruler, especially in situations concerning self-preservation.[64]

Having established the concept of the equality of all men before God and Law, and through this principle the idea that a form of government exists only through the consent of the community, Rutherford proceeded to enumerate the powers of the government and the people as well as their mutual responsibilities. Rutherford acknowledged that, although political power originates from the community, it is treasonous - even satanic - for a private individual to kill a lawful ruler, no matter how tyrannous.[65] Rutherford then examined the parameters of the power received by the ruler once the people approved his rule. As to the abuse of these powers, Rutherford was uncompromising:

> Tyranny being a work of Satan is
> not from God ... the power that

---

[64] Rutherford, Q 13, p. 52; Q 4, p. 6. (See 2 Samuel 12:7-8, Psalms 78:6, Daniel 4:32.)
[65] Rutherford, Q 7, p. 25.

is, must be from God; the magistrate, as magistrate, is good in nature of office, and the intrinsic end of his office, (Rom. xiii.4) for he is the minister of God for thy good; and, therefore, a power ethical, politic, or moral to oppress, is not from God, and is not a power, but a licentious deviation of a power.[66]

In many ways, this was a primary thesis of his book; for Rutherford hoped to demonstrate under what circumstances and conditions the community could resist the civil government. He continued:

The ruler receiveth royal power with the states to make good laws, and power by his royalty to execute those laws, and this power the community hath devolved in the hands of the

---

[66] Rutherford, Q 9, p. 34.

ruler and states of parliament; but the community keepeth to themselves a power to resist tyranny ... We teach not that people should supply all defects in government, nor that they should use their power when anything is done amiss by the ruler ... The people are to suffer much before they resume their power.[67]

Thus, the people could resume their power in extreme circumstances. In the foundation of government, "There is an oath between the ruler and his people, laying on, by reciprocation of bands, mutual civil obligation."[68] Rutherford continued, "the Lord and the people giveth a crown by one and the same action," and using King David as an example he stated: "seeing the people maketh him a ruler covenantwise and conditionally, so he rule

---

[67] Rutherford, Q 9, p. 35-36.
[68] Rutherford, Q 14, p. 54. (See 2 Samuel 5:3, 2 Kings 11:17, Ecclesiastes 8:2.)

according to God's law, and the people resigning their power to him for their safety, and for a peaceable and godly life under him, and not to destroy them, and tyrannize over them."[69] This covenant was presupposed in nature, and thus unwritten, and capable of withstanding a material breach, however "when it is both materially and formally declared by the states to be broken, the people must be free from their allegiance."[70] Therefore, in this, Rutherford began to establish the grounds upon which a nation may lawfully rebel against an unjust government.

After examining the sovereignty of the people in even greater depth, as well as addressing the issue of how lower magistrates are established by God, as well as showing the divine ordination of both legislative and executive power, Rutherford came to the crux of his study with an analysis of the question of whether or not the power given to a ruler is absolute or

---

[69] Rutherford, Q 14, p. 57.
[70] Rutherford, Q 14, p. 61.

limited.[71] He asserted, "God hath given no absolute power to a ruler above the law," and, to summarize, Rutherford offered several primary reasons why this would be so.[72] First, the ruler, as an equal of other humans would be under the law, "The law, rather than the ruler, hath power of life and death."[73] Secondly, "the people have neither formally nor virtually any power absolute to give the ruler ... absolute power above a law is a power to do ill and to destroy the people, and this the people have not themselves ... they cannot give what they never had, and power to destroy themselves they never had."[74] Finally, "All royal power ... is from God. But absolute power to tyrannize over the people and to destroy them is not a power from God; therefore there is not any such royal power absolute." On this premise, Rutherford further reasoned, "if this moral power to sin be from God ... God must be the

---

[71] See also Questions 19-21, pp. 77-99.
[72] Rutherford, Q 22, p. 101. (See Deuteronomy 17:16-20.)
[73] Rutherford, Q 22, p. 102.
[74] Ibid.

author of sin."[75] Thus, Rutherford argued that absolute power, or ambitions to absolute power, was contrary to law, which is above the government; beyond the ability of the people, who did not have such power in themselves to give; and contrary to the nature of God, who, as a law unto himself, could not be the author of sin.

Rutherford expanded this argument by viewing the representatives of the people as above the ruler: "The parliament is co-ordinate ordinarily with the ruler in the power of laws; but the co-ordination on the ruler's part is by derivation, on the parliament's part."[76] Thus, the ruler derived power from parliament, a body that acted as the representatives of the populace. Moreover, the people reserved for themselves the right of self-defense in cases of tyranny. At this point, Rutherford defined a crucially significant term: "A tyrant is he who habitually sinneth against the catholic good of the subjects and state,

---

[75] Ibid.
[76] Rutherford, Q 24, p. 115.

and subverteth law."[77] The most important components of this definition are the word "habitually" and the phrase "subverteth law." Only habitual tyranny warrants lawful resistance, as mentioned above. The addition of the clause concerning law demonstrates how the law, particularly as revealed in the Bible, is above the government. Consequently, the whole concept of "Lex Rex" is a view of how law is king.

As mentioned above, Rutherford espoused the doctrine that the people establish a ruler. Moreover, he also viewed the people as the "fountain of laws."[78] From this dual concept, he concluded, "the ruler by nature is not ruler therefore, he must be ruler by a politic constitution and law from a civil law there is a ruler."[79] Following this statement to its logical conclusion, Rutherford stated, "Because the estates of the rulerdom, who gave him the crown, are above him, they may take

---

[77] Rutherford, Q 24, p. 119.
[78] Rutherford, Q 24, p. 115.
[79] Rutherford, Q 26, p. 126.

away what they gave him; as the law of nature and God saith, If they had known he would turn tyrant, they would never have given him the sword. They gave the power to him only for their good, and that they may make the ruler is clear."[80] Again, that which the people gave the ruler on certain conditional obligations, they have the right to take away when those conditions were not met.

Within the context of the law, Rutherford denied the right of the ruler to be "the sole and final interpreter of law," for this would deny the power of inferior magistrates. In Rutherford's eyes, "the ruler's power of expounding the law is a mere ministerial power, and he hath no dominion of any absolute royal power to expound the law as he will, and to put such a sense of meaning of the law as he pleaseth."[81] Thus, contrary to those who believed in the 'divine right' of kings, Rutherford viewed the king to be under the

---

[80] Rutherford, Q 26, p. 128. (See 2 Chronicles 13:11, 1 Samuel 10:17-24, Deuteronomy 17:14-17.)
[81] Rutherford, Q 27, p. 137.

law and the people. "The king's absolute pleasure can no more be the genuine sense of a just law than his absolute pleasure can be a law ... he is king by, or according to, law, but he is not king of law ... The advancing of any man to the throne, and royal dignity putteth not the man above the number of rational men."[82] Thus, no king is above the law in any way because the very office of king is resultant from the community-established law.

Having established the boundaries within which a government was to be sovereign, Rutherford began the examination of his final point concerning "the lawfulness of resistance in the matter of the king's unjust invasion of life and religion."[83] In keeping with his previous arguments, Rutherford stated: "If the estates of a kingdom give the power to a king, it is their own power in the fountain; and if they give it for their own good, they have power to judge when it is used against

---

[82] Rutherford, Q 27, p. 138.
[83] Rutherford, Q 28, p. 141.

themselves, and for their evil, and so power to limit and resist the power that they gave. ... The people hath ... a power to defend themselves against prodigious cruelty."[84] Rutherford noted the importance of taxation and military power for the maintenance of a country as well as for defense against foreign aggressors; however, when the might of the government turned against the population of a realm, active resistance against such tyranny was essential "as a means of self-preservation."[85] In consideration of this point, Rutherford inquired rhetorically "Since we are not to yield active obedience to all the commandments of superiors, whether they be good or ill ... how is it that we may not deny passive subjection to all the acts of violence exercised?"[86] In other words, if individuals need not obey an unjust command of a ruler, why should

---

[84] Rutherford, Q 28, p. 143.
[85] Rutherford, Q 30, p. 158. (See Q 35, pp. 184-6; Q 44, p. 233.)
[86] Rutherford, Q 30, p. 159.

oppression be met with only non-resistant obedience and no other measures?

At this point, Rutherford espoused a three-fold plan for resisting tyranny. According to Rutherford, "a private man may defend himself against unjust violence, but not in any way he pleaseth the first way is by supplications and apologies."[87] In the modern sense, the first steps of recourse in cases of tyranny are through non-violent means such as the courts, protest, and petitions. If this means proved to be ineffective, Rutherford advocated a second alternative in flight from the country, again without the use of violence in any form. There are two important exceptions to this second option of flight. The first dealt with a situation that witnessed the oppression of a large group. "To a church and a community ... flight is not the second mean, nor a mean at all, because not possible, and therefore not a natural mean of preservation; for the aged, the sick, the suckling infants, and sound religion in the

---

[87] Rutherford, Q 31, p. 160.

posterity cannot flee; flight here is physically, and by nature's necessity, impossible, and therefore no lawful mean."[88] The second exception concerned civil officials, for "Though private men may flee, yet the estates, if they flee, they do not do their duty."[89]

Finally, if these first two options are ineffective, Rutherford determined that the "exigency of the last and most inexorable necessity" is the use of violence, defensively, for the purpose of self-preservation.[90] In closing this argument, asserting the right of self-defense, Rutherford made some statements that parallel the future writings of John Locke concerning the "state of nature." "Nature maketh a man ... even a private man his own judge, magistrate, and defender ... when he hath no judge to give him justice and law. The subjects are to give their lives for the ruler, as the ruler, because the safety of the ruler, as ruler, is the safety of the

---

[88] Ibid.
[89] Rutherford, Q 31, p. 161.
[90] Rutherford, Q 31, p. 160.

commonwealth. But the ruler, as offering unjust violence to his innocent subjects, is not ruler."[91] When the ruler violates his covenant with the people, resulting in tyranny, the population is no longer bound to his rule, although under normal circumstances the subjects are required to lay down their lives for the ruler, albeit the office and not necessarily the person.

Having completed his primary purpose in <u>Lex Rex</u>, Rutherford went on to make some comments about government in general and to reiterate some of his primary points. He first asserted, "An absolute monarchy is not only not the best form of government, but it is the worst."[92] Rutherford was not unreasonable in his statement, and provided several excellent examples for it. "Caesar is great, but law and reason are greater; by an absolute monarchy all things are ruled by will and pleasure above law; then this government cannot be so good as law and reason in a

---

[91] Rutherford, Q 31, p. 164.
[92] Rutherford, Q 38, p. 191.

government by the best, or by many."[93] Although he viewed a limited monarchy, over democracy and aristocracy, as the best form of government, Rutherford stated, "Every government hath something wherein it is best."[94] This is important to note, for while Rutherford developed his ideas in <u>Lex Rex</u> according to the concepts of monarchical rule which were part of the English heritage, his views on government in general contained such broad scope that they could be considered universal in nature, applying to any type of government.

In the institution of monarchy, Rutherford continued his adherence to the simultaneous endowment of power from God and the people through coronation, "so is the office of a ruler immediately instituted of God ... by the mediation of the free consent of the people. ... Because the people hath the royalty radically in themselves, as in the fountain and cause, and conferreth it on the man who is made

---

[93] Ibid.
[94] Rutherford, Q 38, p. 192. (See Q 14, p. 116.)

king."[95] Some of his final comments hinted at an assumed theory of separation of powers between king and parliament. Nevertheless he reemphasized the fact that royal power may be "limited by men," an action which would obviously be pursued through legislative bodies.[96] Rutherford also restated his thoughts concerning the resistance of tyranny, in the collective sense. "Convention of the subjects, in a tumultuary way, for a seditious end, to make war without warrant of law, is forbidden; but not when religion, laws, liberties, invasion of foreign enemies, necessitateth the subjects to convene, though the king and ordinary judicatures, going a corrupt way to pervert judgments, shall refuse to consent to their conventions."[97]

Although Samuel Rutherford has retained a relatively obscure position in history, he was crucial to the development of modern government as a procurer to

---

[95] Rutherford, Q 40, p. 204.
[96] Rutherford, Q 40, pp. 228-9.
[97] Rutherford, Q 44, pp. 232-3.

John Locke. His concern was not to justify a victorious revolution, but as a private citizen interested in the welfare of his country at the risk of his own life. Execution for treason would have probably been his fate, "but ere the time arrived he was summoned to a far higher than an earthly tribunal."[98]   However, his work survived him giving to the world the propositions that all men are equal before God, who appointed government for the maintenance of society and his glory. Using the Bible as the basis for natural law, he viewed the power of government as given by God through the mediation of popular consent. This power was neither absolute nor unconditional.   The community, as the source of civil power, did not have absolute power to give, moreover, knowing the result of such might to be inevitable tyranny, and they would not allow such an extensive grant in any case.   Also, if a ruler where to break covenant with a people, they may, after

---

[98] Rutherford, p. xix.

long patience, rescind the power they had given.

Perhaps the most radical stance of Rutherford was his belief that government is subordinate to the people and law. Any reversal of this balance would result in tyranny, which Rutherford viewed as satanic. In cases of tyranny, the community may resist on the grounds of self-defense and breach of covenant. Establishing grounds for popular resistance, Rutherford enumerated a graduated, three-fold plan of resistance. First, peaceful protests and defenses were to attempt to change the attitudes of the authorities. If this failed, Rutherford recommended flight. However, this was neither feasible nor just for an entire community or lower magistrates. The reason for this was that the movement of a whole group of people would be unfair and dangerous for its weaker members, and for a member of the lower government to flee would be tantamount to desertion of duty. The final option was active resistance, preferably under the supervision of some type of governing body, such as the lower magistrates. This was a last, heinous resort, and to be avoided if possible.

John Locke

Few individuals in history have had influence of comparable stature to John Locke in the area of political theory. Will and Ariel Durant have gone so far as to say, "Locke's influence on political thought remained supreme till Karl Marx."[99] However, contrary to the conclusions of many scholars, Locke was neither the deist nor the great rationalist depicted in subsequent historical inquiry. In fact, as far as political theories were concerned, Locke "was squarely within the mainstream Christian tradition."[100] This is not surprising, considering that Locke's father was "a Puritan attorney, who at some sacrifice supported the parliamentary cause, and expounded to his son the doctrines of popular sovereignty and representative government."[101] Nevertheless, the contributions of Locke to philosophical and political theory, particularly through his

---

[99] Durant, p. 582.
[100] Amos, p. 50.
[101] Durant, p. 576.

<u>Essay Concerning Human Understanding</u> and <u>Second Treatise of Civil Government</u>, have been unparalleled, even to the present.[102]

Writing in defense of the Glorious Revolution, the primary concern of Locke in his <u>Second Treatise</u> was not defending the right of William to the throne, "but (the now victorious) Parliament against any ruler."[103] According to Francis Schaeffer, Locke formulated his theory primarily through "secularizing the Presbyterian tradition ... He stated the results which come from biblical Christianity without having the base which produce them."[104] This is a wholly reasonable statement, because, according to another source, "rationalism ... comes wholly from Locke."[105] Of course, this was not the case entirely, but such a statement does demonstrate the influence that Locke had on subsequent intellectual thought.

---

[102] Engel, p. 241.
[103] Durant, p. 581.
[104] Schaeffer, Vol. 5, p. 138.
[105] Durant, p. 590.

However, the two facts mentioned above have given rise to the belief that Locke was a deist wholly devoid of a Christian worldview, an interpretation particularly expounded by Carl Becker.[106] The formal definition of deism is: "The belief, based solely on reason, in the existence of God as the creator of the universe who after setting it in motion abandoned it, assumed no control over life, exerted no influence on natural phenomena, and gave no supernatural revelation."[107] This system of belief was contrary to what Locke held to be true, for his worldview and beliefs were primarily of Christian extraction. Although described variously as Arian, Socian, and Latitudinarian, "He was not orthodox in all his beliefs, [but] he was far from being a deist."[108]

In examining Locke's work, attention will focus on his views of Christianity as they relate to his theories of government. This is important, because

---

[106] Amos, pp. 50-5.
[107] <u>American Heritage Dictionary</u>: "Deism."
[108] Durant, p. 590; Amos, pp. 56, 145.

Rutherford perceived the Bible as the rule and guide through which to view all knowledge. In addition to this, the similarities between his views of government and those of Rutherford would demonstrate his reliance on Calvinist tradition for his ideas.

The argument often used to support the idea that Locke was devoid of a Protestant heritage concern his Essay Concerning Human Understanding, with particular reference to his doctrine of "tabula rasa." This theory contends, "Our observation employed either, about external sensible objects, or about the internal operations of our minds perceived and reflected on by ourselves, is that which supplies our understandings with all the materials of thinking."[109] In other words, the mind is a blank slate that receives impressions through experience and reflection, and these are the sole basis for the construction of all ideas. Proceeding from this foundation, many scholars have

---

[109] Locke, Essay, 2:1:2.

concluded that Locke was a total devotee to secular philosophy with only deistic references to God. Furthermore, this empirical view is perceived as antithetical to the Christian view of revelation, for the concept of faith involves trusting in what cannot be observed or experienced in the scientific sense. Locke, however, would not have agreed with this interpretation of his theory. As he stated: "Though God has given us no innate ideas of himself ... yet having furnished us with those faculties our mind are endowed with, he hath not left himself without witness: since we have sense, perception, and reason, and cannot want a clear proof of him, as long as we carry ourselves about us."[110]

In another place, Locke stated, "there be no truth that a man may more evidently make out to himself than the existence of a God."[111] Although Locke only noted that reason could show belief in a God (up to this point) even this

---

[110] Ibid, 4:10:1.
[111] Ibid, 1:3:23.

conception was well developed. He viewed God as the "Sovereign Disposer" who ordained the tribulations of this world in order to turn individuals to Himself "with whom there is fullness of joy, and at whose right hand are pleasures for evermore."[112] Moreover, he viewed simple ideas, which are the basis of all knowledge in his epistemology, as ordained by God who has also given men "a mind that can reason."[113] Locke defined reason and faith as follows:

> **Reason** ... I take to be the discovery of the certainty or probability of such propositions or truths, which the mind arrives at by deduction made from such ideas, which it has got by the use of its natural faculties; viz. by sensation or reflection. **Faith** ... is the assent to any proposition, not thus made out by the deductions of reason, but upon

[112] Ibid, 2:7:5 & 6.
[113] Ibid, 4:4:4; 4:17:4.

the credit of the proposer, as coming from God, in some extraordinary way of communication. This way of discovering truths to men, we call **revelation**.[114]

Locke later clarified this statement saying "revelation cannot be admitted against the clear evidence of reason ... Things above reason are, when revealed, the proper matter of faith."[115] In another work of his, Locke stated, "divine revelation receives testimony from no other miracles, but such as are wrought to witness his mission from God who delivers the revelation."[116] Thus, the "deism" of Locke was hardly deistic.

Locke also became more in-depth in his study of the relationship between faith and reason. While he continued to insist that reason was to judge everything, he also maintained, "Whatsoever is divine revelation, ought to overrule all our

[114] Ibid, 4:18:12.
[115] Ibid, 4:18:5 & 7.
[116] Locke, Reasonableness, p. 80.

opinions, prejudices, and interest, and hath a right to be received with full assent. Such a submission as this, of our reason to faith, takes not away the landmarks of knowledge: this shakes not the foundation of reason, but leaves us that use of our faculties for which they were given us."[117] Having made this statement, Locke affirmed what he viewed the divine revelation to be: "The holy Scripture is to me, and always will be, the constant guide of my belief; and I shall always hearken to it, as containing infallible truth relating to things of holy concernment ... God has said it: and I shall immediately condemn and quit any opinion of mine, as soon as I am shown that it is contrary to any revelation in the holy scripture."[118] Thus, Locke considered himself bound to obedience to the Bible as the rule of life. Far from the "clock-maker" mentality of deism, Locke stated, "I am far from denying that God can, or doth sometimes

---

[117] Locke, Essay, 4:18:10.
[118] Amos, p. 55.

enlighten men's minds ... by the immediate influence and assistance of the Holy Spirit."[119]   Locke viewed himself as a Christian.

Most of the citations above, concerning the Christian influence Locke's beliefs were from his <u>Essay Concerning Human Understanding</u>. Most writers who portray Locke as a deist often reference this work specifically. Little mention is ever made of another small book authored by Locke entitled <u>The Reasonableness of Christianity</u>. (In fact, one particular source that discussed Locke would have destroyed its own argument if it had even admitted that the work existed.)[120]   Moreover, the works of Locke, in general, abound with statements concerning God (in a biblical sense) as the supreme good of man. Locke believed individuals are free and subject to "God alone" with regard to this present world.[121]   However, dividing the law of the Old Testament into three

---

[119] Locke, <u>Essay</u>, 4:19:16.
[120] Engel, pp. 239-244.
[121] Locke, <u>Two Tracts</u>, p. 125.

distinct categories, Locke also held every individual responsible to obey the moral Law of Moses, for, "it being a part of the law of nature ... man ought to obey every positive law of God."[122] Admittedly, while neither a Calvinist nor traditional in many respects, Locke was still deeply influenced by Protestant intellectual tradition.   A more exhaustive critique of Locke's religious belief proceeds from an examination of his The <u>Reasonableness of Christianity</u>; however, the examples above will, hopefully, suffice to demonstrate that John Locke, while unorthodox in some ways, grounded his thinking firmly in a Christian worldview nurtured by Protestant beliefs.

While Calvinism did not seem to be prominent in his spiritual thought, many of Locke's arguments concerning government had a solid foundation in Reformed tradition; "This is not to say that Locke was consciously following <u>Lex Rex</u>, but that the argument was well established before

---

[122] Locke, <u>Reasonableness</u>, Sections 22 & 23.

Locke wrote."[123] In his <u>Second Treatise of Civil Government</u>, Locke fully developed his theories of government in order to justify England's Glorious Revolution. He began by referring to his first treatise that undermined the notion that rulers had received their positions as part of the patrimony of Adam. Having shown these views to be false, he gave his definition of political power as: "a right of making laws with penalties of death, and consequently all less penalties, for the regulating and preserving of property, and of employing the force of the community in the execution of such laws, and in the defense of the commonwealth from foreign injury, and all this only for the public good."[124]

Locke proceeded to examine the origins of government. He proposed a theory of circumstances in the early history of man that he termed "the State of Nature." This scenario was "a state of perfect freedom ... within the bounds of

---

[123] Amos, p. 145.
[124] Locke, <u>Treatise</u>, Par. 3.

the law of nature ... a state also of equality."[125]   In answer to the objections that would inevitably come concerning these two terms, Locke turned to Hooker who used the equality of men as "the foundation of that obligation to mutual love amongst men on which he builds the duties they owe one another."[126] Therefore, he viewed equality as based on love and common humanity.   This concept was fundamental for his explanation of liberty inherent in the State of Nature.   Far from equating liberty with anarchy, Locke stated, "though this be a state of liberty, yet it is not a state of license. ... The state of nature has a law of nature to govern it ... and reason, which is that law, teaches all mankind who will but consult it, that, being all equal and independent, no one ought to harm another in his life, health, liberty, or possessions."[127]   Recognizing the drawbacks of this natural state, Locke concluded: "therefore, God hath certainly

---

[125] Ibid, Par. 4.
[126] Ibid, Par. 5.
[127] Ibid, Par. 6.

appointed government to restrain the partiality and violence of men. I easily grant that civil government is the proper remedy for the inconveniences of the state of nature ... And if he that judges, judges amiss in his own or any other case, he is answerable for it to the rest of mankind."[128] Consequently, the State of Nature required the rule of law in order for the continued function of humanity, and Locke viewed this law as ordained by Cod through reason and revelation.[129]

Upon demonstrating that all men are in a State of Nature "til by their own consents they make themselves members of some politic society," Locke emphasized the belief that men are under no authority save by consent.[130] However, this did not give individuals the right to total liberty or slavery. The arguments against license were given above, yet voluntary enslavement was also unacceptable, "For a man not having the power of his own life

---

[128] Ibid, Par. 13.
[129] Locke, Two Tracts, p. 124.
[130] Locke, Treatise, Pars. 15 & 22.

cannot by compact, or his own consent, enslave himself."[131] Although Locke recognized slaves as property, and as such not part of society, he did not condone the voluntary slavery of individuals.[132] Property was an essential concept to Locke because, "God ... hath given the world to men ... to make use of it to the best advantage of life and convenience."[133] To summarize his theory on this, Locke proposed that each individual had, in his own person and labor, property. When a person's labor combines with something other than the individual, that outside influence becomes the property of the one who labored upon it, as long as no waste is produced and enough is left over in common for others to use.[134] While not exhaustive, these are the essentials of his theory of property. For Locke, property was important, because although man was free due to reason, "which is able to

---

[131] Locke, Two Tracts, p. 120; Treatise, Par. 23.
[132] Locke, Treatise, Par. 80.
[133] Ibid, Par. 26.
[134] Ibid, Pars. 27, 31, & 32.

instruct him in that law he is to govern himself by," God made mankind in such a way that "put him under strong obligations of necessity, convenience, and inclination to drive him into society."[135] The reason for this, historically, was that "the several communities settled the bounds of their distinct territories ... regulated the properties of the private men of their society, and so, by compact and agreement, settled the property which labor and industry began."[136] Put another way, the formation of government made properties acquired under the State of Nature official, and this served to regulate the relations between individuals in terms of property.

Locke believed that people have a right to defend their property and, in the context of a civil government, this power was given by society as a whole to those appointed to the duty of protecting the individual members. In his words:

[135] Ibid, Pars. 63 & 77.
[136] Ibid, Pars. 45.

Man being born ... with a title to
perfect freedom ... hath by
nature a power not only to
preserve his property-that is, his
life, liberty, and estate-against
against the injuries and attempts
of other men, but to judge of
and punish the breaches of that
law ... political society, where
every one of the members hath
quitted this natural power,
resigned it up into the hands of
the community in all cases that
exclude him not from appealing
for protection to the law
established by it; ... men
authorized by the community for
their execution, decides all the
differences that may happen
between any members of that
society concerning any matter of
right.[137]

---

[137] Ibid, Par. 87.

This illustrates that in forming a community, according to Locke, the individual concedes his or her rights to the society, and the government as such, to rectify wrongs according to established laws and procedures. In doing this, Locke opposed the formation of absolute monarchies, "For he being supposed to have all, both legislative and executive power in himself alone, there is no judge to be found ... from whence relief and address may be expected of any injury ... suffered from or by his order."[138] In other words, when the ruler has ultimate power there is no legal way for the population to protect themselves from harmful acts perpetrated by the royal power.

For the reasons stated in the above paragraph, Locke figured that societies eventually began to develop representative bodies where "No man ... can be exempted from the laws of it."[139] In such a community, the legislative body possessed

---

[138] Ibid, Par. 91.
[139] Ibid, Par. 94.

"a power to act as one body, which is only by the will and determination of the majority."[140] The community, according to Locke, holds together and is motivated to action by the will of the majority of those who had consented to enter it. With this in mind, he defined the foundation of a political society as "nothing but the consent of any number of freemen capable of a majority to unite and incorporate into such a society."[141]

Having described the establishment of commonwealths in general, Locke proceeded to enumerate the reasons for such an action as well as the responsibilities it entailed. Government arose from the State of Nature because, under the sole rule of natural law, individuals were "constantly exposed to the invasion of others."[142] Locke claimed natural law would have been sufficient to rule humanity "were it not for the corruption and viciousness of degenerate men," but necessity required the

---

[140] Ibid, Par. 96.
[141] Ibid, Par. 99.
[142] Ibid, Par. 123.

formation of civil communities.[143] Furthermore, while society was formed by consent for the protection of property, Locke maintained "By the same act, therefore, whereby any one unites his person, which was before free, to any commonwealth, by the same he unites his possessions, which was before free, to it also; and they become, both of them, person and possession, subject to the government and dominion of that commonwealth as long as it hath being."[144] Those who leave the State of Nature, in doing so, give up themselves, their possessions, liberty and equality to the stewardship of the society, "And all this to be directed to no other end but the peace, safety, and public good of the people."[145] Once the fundamental establishment of government had been confirmed, Locke expanded on this foundation stating, "The majority having ... the whole power of the community, naturally in them, may employ

---

[143] Ibid, Par. 128.
[144] Ibid, Par. 120.
[145] Ibid, Par. 131.

all that power in making laws for the community from time to time, and executing those laws by officers of their own appointing: and ... the community may make compounded and mixed forms of government, as they think good."[146]

While not openly advocating a specific form of government, Locke proposed that there are two distinct branches of government, the legislative, and executive. The former was to determine the law, and the latter was to execute the law. According to Locke, "This legislative is not only the supreme power of the commonwealth, but sacred and unalterable in the hands where the community have once placed it."[147] The representatives of the people were the supreme civil authority; however, this authority was not to condone immoral behavior within the government. After describing several stringent, and yet general, regulations on the powers of the

---

[146] Ibid, Par. 132.
[147] Ibid, Par. 134.

legislative portion of government, Locke encapsulated his views concerning the legislative power saying, "the legislative power is put into the hands of divers persons who duly assembled, have by themselves or jointly with others a power to make laws, which when they have done they are themselves subject to ... which is a new and near tie upon them, to take care that they make them for the public good."[148]

In addition to the legislative, Locke also conceived of an executive power that he held responsible for "the execution of the municipal laws of the society within itself upon all that are parts of it."[149] Incidentally, he combined this power with a so-called federative power responsible for the management of relations with other societies. Locke believed that "the executive is vested in a single person, who had power that was derived from the people via the legislature, and thus

---

[148] Ibid, Par. 143.
[149] Ibid, Par. 147.

subordinate to both."[150] Moreover, as with the legislative arm of governing power, "princes ... owe subjection to the laws of God and Nature. No body, no power, can exempt them from the obligations of that eternal law."[151] Therefore, although there were certain matters "left to the discretion of him that has the executive power," both ruler and legislature had the primary responsibility of remaining within the bounds of natural and divine law, thus allowing no one to be above the law.[152] This was an essential point that would define when a government had become tyrannical and thus eligible for dissolution by the community that had given it power.

Locke defined tyranny as "the exercise of power beyond right for ... private separate advantage."[153] Using quotations from King James to support his definition, Locke observed that any form of government is liable to tyranny through

---

[150] Ibid, Par. 151.
[151] Ibid, Par. 195.
[152] Ibid, Par. 159.
[153] Ibid, Par. 199.

the violation of law. "Wherever law ends tyranny begins, if the law be transgressed to another's harm."[154] His later comments explained that force should oppose the unlawful commands of a prince.[155] To support this position, Locke relied on the concepts he had developed earlier, and stated, "For the ruler's authority being given him only by the law, he cannot empower any one to act against the law."[156] However, he also commented, "the right of resisting, even in such manifest acts of tyranny, will not suddenly or on slight occasions disturb the government ... if it reach no farther than some private men's cases."[157] Nevertheless, Locke concluded, since a ruler's office was created by and under law, if his breaches of law were to threaten the greater part of society resistance would be lawful. Like Rutherford, Locke supported this because

---

[154] Ibid, Par. 202.
[155] Ibid, Par. 203-204.
[156] Ibid, Par. 206.
[157] Ibid, Par. 208.

the people were entitled to take away the power they previously gave.[158]

Finally, Locke considered the dissolution of government. He considered this a right in situations that saw the legislature "broken or dissolved." He reasoned that, "The constitution of the legislature is the first and fundamental act of the society, whereby provision is made for the continuation of their union, under the direction of persons and bonds of laws made by persons authorized thereunto by the consent and appointment of the people."[159] In such a situation, Locke stated, "the people are at liberty to provide for themselves by erecting a new legislature ... for their safety and good."[160] According to Locke, "The end of government is the good of mankind," which he considered the preservation of the property of individuals from harm.[161] Thus, whenever the legislative or executive branch of

---

[158] Ibid, Par. 209-210.

[159] Ibid, Par. 212.

[160] Ibid, Par. 220.

[161] Ibid, Par. 229.

government "endeavor to invade the property of the subject ... or to reduce them to slavery," the trust between the people and government has been violated, and the people are entitled to reclaim the power they had originally entrusted to the civil authorities.[162] Locke placed the responsibility in the people to determine when their trust had been violated, and "If a controversy arises ... of great consequence ... the proper umpire in such a case should be the body of the people."[163] Locke concluded his treatise with this affirmation that the population must be subject to the governing authorities. However, if the government were to forfeit its political power, "it reverts back to society, and the people have a right to act as supreme, and continue the legislative in themselves; or place it in a new form, or hands as they think good."[164] Concluding from where he began, Locke reaffirmed that popular consent is the root of all political power.

---

[162] Ibid, Par. 221-2.
[163] Ibid, Par. 242; 240.
[164] Ibid, Par. 243.

John Locke was one of the most influential philosophers in history. His studies included a variety of areas from education to epistemology to political thought. Contrary to the opinions of many recent scholars, Locke did not hold to a deistic view of the world. Rather, the general Protestant heritage of his culture primarily influenced Locke, even if several of his beliefs were unorthodox and even heretical. Locke believed faith should enhance reason, a concept clearly stated in his Essay Concerning Human Understanding. In the context of his political theory, Locke was the direct intellectual descendant of Reformed Protestantism. The many similarities between his Second Treatise of Civil Government and Lex Rex, published almost fifty years earlier, illustrate this.

According to Locke, the purpose of civil government is to make and execute laws for the preservation of property and the public good. He described humanity, prior to the formation of political society, as in a State of Nature. In this state, all men stood as free and equal under the laws of nature, however this situation was one of insecurity due to the depravity of man. In order to restrain the partiality and violence of men, according to Locke, God appointed civil government, and formed it through the consent of the people. Once formed, government was to protect the property of those governed. He broadly defined property as a result of the mixture of resources and labor. Locke found absolute monarchy to be an unfavorable form of government, for in that situation the ruler, who would be supreme lawmaker, would simultaneously be the highest judicial authority, a system with clear opportunities for abuse. In contrast to this, Locke proposed that the office of ruler was a creation of the legislative power, which had in turn been created by the people and thus responsible to the will of the majority. Furthermore, Locke placed all offices of power, whether legislative or executive, under constraints of obedience to the Laws of God and Nature, thus allowing no one to be above the law. Having established that the population is the supreme repository of power, Locke concluded the grant of power given by them to the civil authorities is revocable in cases when the majority of society was threatened.

Thomas Jefferson

Having examined the political thought that preceded the American Revolution through the studies of Calvin, Rutherford, and Locke, this investigation shall conclude with the primary author of the Declaration of Independence, Thomas Jefferson. Jefferson has been chosen as the final subject for examination for several reasons, the most prominent being that as a virulent opponent of Calvinism his concurrence with Reformed political tradition would demonstrate the great influence of Reformed thought on the formation of the United States as a whole. While this assertion may seem radical to some scholars, theistic principles have an important part of American political thinking. According to one author, the entire system of government in America and England proceeded from "a stratum of the Old Testament teaching derived through the Puritan Revolution."[165]

---

[165] Friedenwald, p. 206.

However, even this assertion pales in comparison to that of Oscar S. Straus who believed the American Federal Republican system was the fulfillment of the ancient Hebrew commonwealth.[166] Thus, this evidence would tend to accentuate the assertion that thought linked to the Puritan tradition was of greater value than Enlightenment philosophy in the formation of the principles, which led to the American Revolution.

In comparison with the three former case studies already mentioned, this study of Jefferson shall not be nearly as extensive. Actually, this section more a concluding statement rather than a case study per se. For the purposes of this examination, a study of the Declaration of Independence shall suffice, with additional material and commentary cited as necessary. A comprehensive investigation of Jefferson's political theory is difficult because, "His theories were not combined in any single

---

[166] Staus, 1885.

treatise."[167]   However, the Declaration provides a good summation of his political thought, at least in the colonial period. In addition, his Summary View of the Rights of British America from 1774 also demonstrates the direction of his thinking concerning the colonies. The importance of Jefferson was not in his original thought; rather it was in his application of accepted principles that made him prominent. According to Charles M. Wiltse: "Jefferson's influence was all out of proportion to his intellectual contributions. He was not an original thinker but his unique time and place ... made him the instrument of giving practical application to the ideas of others. It was through Jefferson that the political liberalism of accumulated centuries passed into the democratic tradition."[168] Nevertheless, the Declaration of Independence was a true watershed in American and European history, bringing "the speculations of

---

[167] Gettell, p. 195.
[168] DeJong, p.32.

political philosophers down from the heights of theory into the arena of practical politics. It proclaimed its principles of liberty ... and stirred men anew to investigate the foundations of political life."[169]

In writing the Declaration of Independence, Jefferson faced a true dilemma because, as he later stated, "it was intended to be an expression of the American mind."[170] Beginning as an expression of "ultimate values," the Declaration hoped to fulfill several goals for the immediate and distant future.[171] As a foundational document, occasioned by the secession of the thirteen colonies from England, "Jefferson wished to have ... for the future the broadest possible statement of the rights of men as individuals and citizens."[172] Nevertheless, he also had far more urgent matters to address. Domestically, the Continental Congress

---

[169] Gettell, p. 96.
[170] Brodie, p. 143.
[171] Whitehead, p. 75.
[172] Tyler, p. 8.

was in need of "a popular document ... to impress the masses, to place before the young nation at its birth a certain ideal and a certain political faith."[173] Moreover, on the international scene, the Declaration of Independence was "a shrewd step in diplomacy, making possible aid from those European countries that wished to weaken England, and which would help the colonies to separate themselves from the mother country."[174] Thus, while Jefferson was required to produce a document steeped in ideology, his considerations of the practical situation also played a great role in his work as a writer.

The real issue for many historians, concerning the Declaration of Independence, is the type of philosophy of life or Weltanschauung that this document represents. Many cite the influence of Calvin, according to one source, "He that will not honor the memory and respect the influence of Calvin knows but little of the

---

[173] DeJong, p. 16.
[174] Gettell, p. 96.

origin of American independence."[175] Often, Jefferson is alleged, due to his deism, to hold political views diametrically opposed to the tenets of Calvinism. There is a great wealth of information to demonstrate that Jefferson "loathed Calvinists and rejected their belief in a sovereign, providential God who was directly involved in mapping the course of history," but this did not mean he was contemptuous of all things and people related to Calvin, as his great correspondence with John Adams demonstrated.[176] Actually, with regard to his public life, "Jefferson was sensitive both personally and politically to the views of others and was therefore normally reticent in expressing his convictions."[177] Despite this, a whole school of thought has risen linking the ideological roots of the Declaration of Independence solely to "the eighteenth-century Enlightenment."[178]

---

[175] McFetridge, p. 69.
[176] DeJong, p. 34.
[177] Miller, p. 25.
[178] Wells, p.124.

This interpretation is erroneous, for the ideology of the Declaration of Independence was the direct fruition of Reformed political theory and tradition.

When the time came for the Continental Congress to choose an individual to draft the Declaration, Jefferson was called, "with singular unanimity, as the one best fitted by his attainments to produce a document of the charter desired."[179] This decision was based upon the past experience of Jefferson as the author of A Summary View of the Rights of British America in 1774, which had been meant to serve the dual purpose of educating Virginian delegates of the issues to be addressed in that year, as well as to provide a common ground from which the Congress could pursue various options.[180] In this document, Jefferson appealed to the king for redress of the colonial grievances while reminding the him: "that he is no more

---

[179] Friedenwald, p. 173.
[180] Ibid.

than the chief officer of the people, appointed by laws, and circumscribed with definite powers, to assist in working the great machine of government, erected for their use, and, consequently, subject to their superintendence ... from the origin and first settlement of these countries."[181] From the outset, Jefferson argued from a position of popular sovereignty, and even reminded the king of precedent in English history when: "A Family of princes was ... on the throne, whose treasonable crimes against their people brought on them, afterwards, the exertion of those sacred and sovereign rights of punishment, reserved in the hands of the people for extreme necessity, and judged by the constitution unsafe to be delegated to any other judicature."[182]

After enumerating the acts of tyranny which had, up to that time, been perpetrated against the colonies, Jefferson stated: "Single acts of tyranny may be

---

[181] Jefferson, p. 6.
[182] Ibid., p. 7.

ascribed to the accidental opinion of a day; but a series of oppressions ... too plainly prove a deliberate, systematical plan of reducing us to slavery."[183] After, again, elaborating on the gravity of the situation with particular reference to Parliament and the king, Jefferson ended with a plea:

> These are our grievances, which we have thus laid before his Majesty, with that freedom of language and sentiment, which becomes a free people, claiming their rights as derived from the laws of nature, and not as the gift of their Chief Magistrate. ... This, Sire, is our last, determined resolution. And that you will be pleased to interpose with that efficacy which your earnest endeavors may insure, to procure redress of these our great grievances, to quiet the minds of your subjects ... is the

---

[183] Ibid., p. 10.

fervent prayer of all British America.[184]

Being "too advanced" for its time, the Summary View was not taken into consideration by the Congress of 1774, but in this essay, Jefferson "touched upon every phase of the colonial contentions, and thereby established his reputation as a forceful, sagacious, philosophical thinker."[185]   Therefore, Jefferson was an obvious choice to author the Declaration summarizing the argument he made for the colonies in his former work.

In an incredibly short period, Jefferson had concluded his draft and submitted it to the Congress.   From that point, he patiently watched as the entire Continental Congress discussed his document, making alterations and revisions.   Jefferson thus described the principle changes enacted by this discussion:

---

[184] Ibid, pp. 18-19.
[185] Friedenwald, p. 174.

The pusillanimous idea that we had friends in England worth making terms with still haunted the minds of many. For this reason those passages which conveyed censures on the people of England were struck out, lest they should give them offence. The clause, too, reprobating enslaving the inhabitants of Africa, was struck out in complaisance to South Carolina and Georgia, who had never attempted to restrain the importation of slaves ... Our Northern brethren also I believe felt a little tender under these censures.[186]

Nevertheless, the final draft of the Declaration of Independence revealed the will of the Congress as a whole. Mention should be made here of the line of thought,

---

[186] Ibid, p. 130.

speaking of Calvinism in particular, leading to the concepts enumerated in the Declaration. Calvin, as the virtual originator of Reformed thought, demonstrated the principles that stand at the foundation of Calvinist political theory. Subsequently, Rutherford brought forth the maturation of Puritan political theories, which were similar to Jefferson in a multitude of ways. After this, Locke provided the intellectual bridge between Jefferson and the late Reformation. Finally, the work of Jefferson, as amended by the Continental Congress, was a culmination of the Reformed thought that preceded it.

The preamble of the Declaration stated an explanation for its creation as a document: "When, in the course of human events, it becomes necessary for one people to dissolve the political bands which have connected them with another ... a decent respect to the opinions of mankind requires that they should declare the causes which impel them to the separation."[187] This

---

[187] Amos, 171-175.

desire for documented justification for social and political action was reflected in Calvin, who stated, "in human transactions some procedure is always in effect, which is to be respected in the interests of public decency, and even of humanity itself."[188] In other words, the colonies could not simply proclaim their independence for no reason at all; rather they were required to justify their action before the community and the world.

Having established the reasons for vocalizing the intentions of the colonists, Jefferson proceeded to introduce their philosophical justification, stating "We hold these truths to be self-evident..." and enumerating those truths. The first proposition was "that all men are created equal." Calvin did not give great examination to this concept, except for some vague statements such as, "Equity, because it is natural, cannot but be the same for all, and ... this same purpose ought to apply to all laws, whatever their

---

[188] Calvin, Institutes, IV.x.27.

object."[189] Rutherford, on the other hand, taking into consideration the nature of mankind as sinful creatures, was quite comfortable saying, "all men are born alike and equal."[190]

In addition to equality, the Declaration viewed mankind as "endowed, by their Creator, with certain unalienable rights; that among these are life, liberty, and the pursuit of happiness to secure these rights, governments are instituted among men." This statement affirmed the concept of natural law and described the role of government as the protector and upholder of this law. Natural law was an important tenet in the thought of Calvin who defined it as "that apprehension of the conscience which distinguishes sufficiently between just and unjust, and which deprive men of the excuse of ignorance."[191] In terms of law, Rutherford stated, "God hath immediately by the law of nature appointed their should be a government," thus in

---

[189] Ibid, IV.xx.16.
[190] Rutherford, Q 7, p. 25.
[191] Calvin, Institutes, II.ii.22.

keeping with the thought of the Declaration which viewed all rights as "endowed" by the Creator."[192] Moreover, Calvin and Rutherford viewed government as the instrument that protected the rights of the people. According to Calvin, "civil government does not merely see to it ... that men breathe, eat, drink, and are kept warm ... it provides that each man may keep his property safe and sound; that men may carry blameless intercourse among themselves; that honesty and modesty may be preserved among men."[193] Rutherford similarly stated, "It is lawful to repel violence by violence; and this is a special act of the magistrate."[194] Thus, both Calvin and Rutherford viewed the establishment of government as an institute of natural law to protect the rights of the populace.

The third concept voiced by the Declaration asserted that governments derive "their just power from the consent of the governed." This also was a

---

[192] Rutherford, Q 2, p. 3.
[193] Calvin, Institutes, IV.xx.3.
[194] Rutherford, Q 2, p. 3.

prevalent stream in Puritan thought. Calvin, citing Church history, wrote "In ancient times no one was even received into the assembly of clergy without the consent of all the people."[195] With this fundamental concept established in the Presbyterian method of church order, Rutherford was able to apply it to civil government as well. Concerning the Parliament, or legislative branch, "The estates taken collectively do represent the people both in respect of office, and of persons, because they stand judges for them."[196] With regard for the king, or executive branch, "the king is inferior to the people; have they a fountain-power above him, because they made him king."[197] Therefore, Reformed thought viewed the people as the repository of power long before the age of the Enlightenment.

Since the people are the root power of civil government, this logically dictates that an oppressive government is

---

[195] Calvin, Institutes, IV.iv.10.
[196] Rutherford, Q 21, p. 99.
[197] Ibid, Q 19, p. 83.

illegitimate, and liable for dissolution. In the language of the Declaration: "whenever any form of government becomes destructive ... it is the right of the people to alter or abolish it, and to institute new government, laying its foundation on such principles, and organizing its powers in such form, as to them shall seem most likely to effect their safety and happiness." Calvin, in a similar vein, declared:

> If there are now any magistrates of the people, appointed to restrain the willfulness of kings ... I am so far from forbidding them to withstand, in accordance with their duty, the fierce licentiousness of kings, that, if they wink at kings who violently fall upon and assault the lowly common folk, I declare that their dissimulation involves nefarious perfidy.[198]

---

[198] Calvin, Institutes, IV.xx.31.

Rutherford, in gentler terms, stated, "The king receiveth royal power with the states to make good laws, and power by his royalty to execute laws, and this power the community hath devolved in the hands of the king and states of parliament; but the community keepeth to themselves a power to resist tyranny, and to coerce it."[199]

In addition, all three of these thinkers agreed that, in the language of the Declaration, "governments long established, should not be changed for light and transient causes." Jefferson expanded on this statement, noting, "when a long train of abuses and usurpations ... evinces a design to reduce them under absolute despotism ... it is their duty to throw off such a government." Calvin counseled patience under "imperious domination."[200] Likewise, Rutherford's council of patience a tyrant, which he defined as "he who habitually sinneth against the catholic good of the subjects and state, and subverteth

---

[199] Rutherford, Q 9, p. 35.
[200] Calvin, <u>Institutes</u>, II.ii.24.

law." Following the model Rutherford proposed for civil resistance, the Declaration, having made its accusations toward England, sought to prove its allegations by letting facts "be submitted to a candid world." These facts demonstrated the tyranny of England thoroughly, in full keeping with the definition of Rutherford, and determined that George III was "unfit to be the ruler of a free people."[201]

The Declaration proceeded to state, "Nor have we been wanting in attentions to our British brethren. We have warned them, from time to time, of attempts by their legislature to extend an unwarranted jurisdiction over us." In doing this, the colonies had followed the model for resistance endorsed by Rutherford. With the failure of the initial steps of "supplications and apologies," and with flight an impossibility, the Continental Congress was forced to enact their final option of "violent re-offending" to protect their territories from the tyranny of the

---

[201] Rutherford, Q 24, p. 119.

king.[202]   Rutherford further bolstered the American cause, in particular reference to the legality of the Continental Congress, with such statements as: "Convention of the subjects, in a tumultuary way, ... is forbidden; but not when religion, laws, liberties, invasion of foreign enemies, necessitateth the subjects to convene, though the king and ordinary judicatures, going a corrupt way to pervert judgment, shall refuse to consent to their conventions."[203] According to Calvinistic political thought, the colonies were justified and appropriate in their actions.

The Declaration closed stating that the Congress "by authority of the good people of these colonies, solemnly publish and declare, That these United Colonies are, and of right ought to be free and independent states." From this point, there could be no turning back for the colonists, in the words of Rutherford: "The covenant may be materially broken, while the king

---

[202] Ibid, Q 31, pp. 159-61.
[203] Ibid, Q 44, pp. 232-3.

remaineth king, and the subjects remain subjects; but when it is both materially and formally declared by the states to be broken, the people must be free from their allegiance."[204] Thus, while Rutherford may not have been prominent in the thought of the actual framers of the Declaration of Independence, their actions were in astute keeping with his theories propounded in Lex Rex. As has been shown, through the mediation of Locke, the Reformed thought of Calvin and Rutherford was crucial to the political principles applied in the Declaration of Independence, written by Jefferson with slight revisions by the Continental Congress. Therefore, the ideology that served to produce the American Revolution was not the product of Enlightenment philosophies, but rather of the Calvinistic-Reformed-Puritan traditions of England and America that predated the philosophies by over one hundred years.

---

[204] Ibid, Q 14, p. 61.

BIBLIOGRAPHY

Primary Sources

Calvin, John. A Commentary on Daniel.
Edinburgh: The Banner of Truth
Trust, 1561 (1986).

Calvin, John. John T. McNeill, Ed.
Institutes of the Christian Religion.
Philadelphia: The Westminster Press,
1559 (1960).

Dillenberger, John. John Calvin. Garden
City: Double Day and Co., 1971.

Jefferson, Thomas. Saul K. Pandover Ed.
The Complete Jefferson. New York:
Duell, Shawn & Pearce Inc. 1943.

Jefferson, Thomas. Merrill D. Peterson ed.
Thomas Jefferson: Writings. New
York: The Library of America, 1984.

Locke, John. Robert Hutchins Ed. An
Essay Concerning Human
Understanding. Chicago:
Encyclopedia Britannica Inc. 1952.

Locke, John. Charles L. Sherman Ed.
Second Treatise of Civil

Government. New York: Appleton-Century-Crofts, 1937.

Locke, John. I.T. Ramsey Ed. The Reasonableness of Christianity and A Discourse Concerning Miracles. Stanford: Stanford University Press, 1958.

Locke, John. Philip Abrams Ed. Two Tracts on Civil Government. Cambridge: Cambridge University Press, 1967.

Manschreck, Clyde L. Ed. A History of Christianity. Ann Arbor: Prentice Hall Inc., 1964.

Rutherford, Samuel. Lex Rex, or The Law and the King. Harrisonburg: Sprinkle Publications, 1644 (1982).

Williamson, G.I. The Westminster Confession of Faith for Study Classes. Philipsburg: Presbyterian and Reformed Publishing, 1964.

Secondary Sources

American Heritage Dictionary, 1985 Ed.

Amos, Gary T. Defending the Declaration. Brentwood: Wolgemuth &Hyatt Publishers Inc., 1989.

Armstrong, William Ed. Calvin and the Reformation. Grand Rapids: Baker Book House, 1988.

Becker, Carl L., The Heavenly City of the Eighteenth-Century Philosophers. New Haven: Yale University Press, 1932.

The Bible. King James Version.

Bouwsma, William J. John Calvin. New York: Oxford University Press, 1988.

Brodie, Fawn M. Thomas Jefferson. New York: Bantam Books Inc., 1974.

Cunningham, William. The Reformers and the Theology of the Reformation. Edinburgh: The Banner of Truth Trust, 1862 (1989).

DeJong, Norman. Christianity and Democracy. USA: The Craig Press, 1978.

Durant, Will & Ariel. <u>The Age of Louis XIV. Vol. 8</u>. The Story of Civilization. New York: Simon and Schuster, 1963.

Engel, S. Morris. <u>The Study of Philosophy</u>. San Diego: Collegiate Press, 1987.

Finnis, John. <u>Natural Law and Natural Rights</u>. Oxford: Claredon Press, 1980.

Fisher, George P. <u>The Reformation</u>. New York: Scribner, Armstrong and Co., 1874.

Friedenwald, Herbert. <u>The Declaration of Independence</u>. New York: The Macmillan Co., 1904.

George, Timothy. <u>Theology of the Reformers</u>. Nashville: Broadman Press, 1988.

Gettell, Raymond G. <u>History of American Political Thought</u>. New York: Appleton-Century-Crofts Inc., 1928.

McFetridge, N.S. <u>Calvinism in History</u>. St. Edmonton: Still Waters Revival Books, 1882 (1989).

Miller, Charles. _Jefferson and Nature_. Baltimore: Johns Hopkins University Press, 1988.

Parker, T.H.L. _John Calvin_. England: Lion Publishing, 1975.

Schaeffer, Francis A. _The Complete Works of Francis A. Schaeffer 5 Vol_. Westchester: Crossway Books, 1982.

Straus, Oscar. _The Origin of Republican Form of Government in the United States of America_. New York: The Knickerbocker Press, 1885 (1926).

Tyler, Alice Felt. _Freedom's Ferment_. New York: Harper Row, 1944.

Wells, Peter. _The American War of Independence_. London: University of London Press, 1967.

Wendel, Frangois. _Calvin_. London: William Collins and Sons, and Co., 1963.

Whitehead, John W. _The Second American Revolution_. Westchester: Crossway Books, 1982.

Wills, Gary. _Inventing America_. Garden City: Doubleday, 1978.

APPENDIX A

WESTMINSTER CONFESSION OF FAITH (1643-47) CHAPTER 23 OF THE CIVIL MAGISTRATE

1. God, the supreme Lord and King of all the world, hath ordained civil magistrates, to be, under him, over the people, for his own glory, and the public good: and, to this end, hath armed them with the power of the sword, for the defense and encouragement of them that do good, and for the punishment of evil doers.

2. It is lawful for Christians to accept and execute the office of a magistrate, when called thereunto: in the managing whereof, as they ought especially to maintain piety, justice, and peace, according to the wholesome laws of each commonwealth: so, for that end, they may lawfully, now under the new testament,

wage war, upon just and necessary occasion.

3. Civil magistrates may not assume to themselves the administration of the Word and sacraments; or the power of the keys of the kingdom of heaven; or, in the least, interfere in matters of faith. Yet, as nursing fathers, it is the duty of civil magistrates to protect the church of our common Lord, without giving the preference to any denomination of Christians above the rest, in such a manner that all ecclesiastical persons whatever shall enjoy the full, free, unquestioned liberty of discharging every part of their sacred function, without violence or danger. And, as Jesus Christ hath appointed a regular government and discipline in his church, no law of any commonwealth should interfere with, let, or hinder, the due exercise thereof, among the voluntary members of any denominations of Christians, according to their own profession and belief. It is the duty of civil magistrates to protect the person and good

name of all their people, in such an effectual manner as that no person be suffered, either upon pretense of religion or infidelity, to offer any indignity, violence, abuse, or injury to any other person whatsoever: and to take order, that all religious and ecclesiastical assemblies be held without molestation or disturbance.

4. It is the duty of people to pray for magistrates, to honor their persons, to pay them tribute or other dues, to obey their lawful commands, and to be subject to their authority, for conscience sake. Infidelity, or difference in religion, doth not make void the magistrates just and legal authority, nor free the people from their due obedience to them: from which ecclesiastical persons are not exempted, much less hath the pope any power and jurisdiction over them in their dominions, or over any of their people; and least of all, to deprive them of their dominions, or lives, if he shall judge them to be heretics, or upon any other pretense whatsoever.

APPENDIX B

The Declaration of Independence

A Transcription

IN CONGRESS, July 4, 1776.

The unanimous Declaration of the thirteen United States of America,

When in the Course of human events, it becomes necessary for one people to dissolve the political bands which have connected them with another, and to assume among the powers of the earth, the separate and equal station to which the Laws of Nature and of Nature's God entitle them, a decent respect to the opinions of mankind requires that they should declare the causes which impel them to the separation.

We hold these truths to be self-evident, that all men are created equal, that they are endowed by their Creator with certain unalienable Rights, that among these are Life, Liberty and the pursuit of Happiness. --That to secure these rights, Governments are instituted among Men, deriving their just powers from the consent of the governed, --That whenever any Form of Government becomes destructive of these ends, it is the Right of the People to alter or to abolish it, and to institute new Government, laying its foundation on such principles and organizing its powers in such form, as to them shall seem most likely to effect their Safety and Happiness. Prudence, indeed, will dictate that Governments long established should not be changed for light and transient causes; and accordingly all experience hath shewn, that mankind are more disposed to suffer, while evils are sufferable, than to right themselves by abolishing the forms to which they are accustomed. But when a long train of abuses and usurpations, pursuing invariably the same Object evinces a design to reduce them under absolute Despotism, it is their right, it is their duty, to throw off such Government, and to provide new Guards for their future security. --Such has been the patient sufferance of these Colonies; and such is now the necessity which constrains them to alter their former Systems of Government. The history of the present King of Great Britain is a history of repeated injuries and usurpations, all having in direct object the establishment of an absolute Tyranny over these States. To prove this, let Facts be submitted to a candid world.

He has refused his Assent to Laws, the most wholesome and necessary for the public good.

He has forbidden his Governors to pass Laws of immediate and pressing importance unless suspended in their operation till his Assent should be obtained; and when so suspended, he has utterly neglected to attend to them.

He has refused to pass other Laws for the accommodation of large districts of people, unless those people would relinquish the right of Representation in the Legislature, a right inestimable to them and formidable to tyrants only.

He has called together legislative bodies at places unusual, uncomfortable, and distant from the depository of their public Records, for the sole purpose of fatiguing them into compliance with his measures.

He has dissolved Representative Houses repeatedly, for opposing with manly firmness his invasions on the rights of the people.

He has refused for a long time, after such dissolutions, to cause others to be elected; whereby the Legislative powers, incapable of Annihilation, have returned to the People at large for their exercise; the State remaining in the mean time exposed to all the dangers of invasion from without, and convulsions within.

He has endeavoured to prevent the population of these States; for that purpose obstructing the Laws for Naturalization of

Foreigners; refusing to pass others to encourage their migrations hither, and raising the conditions of new Appropriations of Lands.

He has obstructed the Administration of Justice, by refusing his Assent to Laws for establishing Judiciary powers.

He has made Judges dependent on his Will alone, for the tenure of their offices, and the amount and payment of their salaries.

He has erected a multitude of New Offices and sent hither swarms of Officers to harrass our people, and eat out their substance.

He has kept among us, in times of peace, Standing Armies without the Consent of our legislatures.

He has affected to render the Military independent of and superior to the Civil power.

He has combined with others to subject us to a jurisdiction foreign to our constitution, and unacknowledged by our laws; giving his Assent to their Acts of pretended Legislation:

For Quartering large bodies of armed troops among us:

For protecting them, by a mock Trial, from punishment for any Murders which they should commit on the Inhabitants of these States:

For cutting off our Trade with all parts of the world:

For imposing Taxes on us without our Consent:

For depriving us in many cases, of the benefits of Trial by Jury:

For transporting us beyond Seas to be tried for pretended offences

For abolishing the free System of English Laws in a neighbouring Province, establishing therein an Arbitrary government, and enlarging its Boundaries so as to render it at once an example and fit instrument for introducing the same absolute rule into these Colonies:

For taking away our Charters, abolishing our most valuable Laws, and altering fundamentally the Forms of our Governments:

For suspending our own Legislatures, and declaring themselves invested with power to legislate for us in all cases whatsoever.

He has abdicated Government here, by declaring us out of his Protection and waging War against us.

He has plundered our seas, ravaged our Coasts, burnt our towns, and destroyed the lives of our people.

He is at this time transporting large Armies of foreign Mercenaries to complete the works of death, desolation and tyranny, already begun with circumstances of Cruelty & perfidy scarcely paralleled in the most barbarous ages, and totally unworthy the Head of a civilized nation.

He has constrained our fellow Citizens taken Captive on the high Seas to bear Arms against their Country, to become the executioners of their friends and Brethren, or to fall themselves by their Hands.

He has excited domestic insurrections amongst us, and has endeavoured to bring on the inhabitants of our frontiers, the merciless Indian Savages, whose known rule of warfare, is an undistinguished destruction of all ages, sexes and conditions.

In every stage of these Oppressions We have Petitioned for Redress in the most humble terms: Our repeated Petitions have been answered only by repeated injury. A Prince whose character is thus marked by every act which may define a Tyrant, is unfit to be the ruler of a free people.

Nor have We been wanting in attentions to our British brethren. We have warned them from time to time of attempts by their legislature to extend an unwarrantable jurisdiction over us. We have reminded them of the circumstances of our emigration and settlement here. We have appealed to their native justice and magnanimity, and we have conjured them by the ties of our common kindred to disavow these usurpations, which, would inevitably interrupt our connections and correspondence. They too have been deaf to the voice of justice and of consanguinity. We must, therefore, acquiesce in the necessity, which denounces our Separation, and hold them, as we hold the rest of mankind, Enemies in War, in Peace Friends.

We, therefore, the Representatives of the united States of America, in General Congress, Assembled, appealing to the Supreme Judge of the world for the rectitude of our intentions, do, in the Name, and by Authority of the good People of these Colonies, solemnly publish and declare, That these United Colonies are, and of Right ought to be Free and Independent States; that they are Absolved from all Allegiance to the British Crown, and that all political connection between them and the State of Great Britain, is and ought to be totally dissolved; and that as Free and Independent States, they have full Power to levy War, conclude Peace, contract Alliances, establish Commerce, and to do all other Acts and Things which Independent States may of right do. And for the support of this Declaration, with a firm reliance on the protection of divine Providence, we mutually pledge to each other our Lives, our Fortunes and our sacred Honor.

The 56 signatures on the Declaration appear in the positions indicated:

[Column 1]
Georgia:
Button Gwinnett
Lyman Hall
George Walton
[Column 2]
North Carolina:
William Hooper
Joseph Hewes
John Penn
South Carolina:

Edward Rutledge
Thomas Heyward, Jr.
Thomas Lynch, Jr.
Arthur Middleton
[Column 3]
Massachusetts:
John Hancock
Maryland:
Samuel Chase
William Paca
Thomas Stone

Charles Carroll of
Carrollton
Virginia:
George Wythe
Richard Henry Lee
Thomas Jefferson
Benjamin Harrison
Thomas Nelson, Jr.
Francis Lightfoot Lee
Carter Braxton
[Column 4]
Pennsylvania:
Robert Morris
Benjamin Rush
Benjamin Franklin
John Morton
George Clymer
James Smith
George Taylor
James Wilson
George Ross
Delaware:
Caesar Rodney
George Read
Thomas McKean
[Column 5]
New York:
William Floyd

Philip Livingston
Francis Lewis
Lewis Morris
New Jersey:
Richard Stockton
John Witherspoon
Francis Hopkinson
John Hart
Abraham Clark
[Column 6]
New Hampshire:
Josiah Bartlett
William Whipple
Massachusetts:
Samuel Adams
John Adams
Robert Treat Paine
Elbridge Gerry
Rhode Island:
Stephen Hopkins
William Ellery
Connecticut:
Roger Sherman
Samuel Huntington
William Williams
New Hampshire:
Matthew Thornton

Also from Woodbine Cottage Publications:

E-mail us for special discount pricing at:
awcpublications@aol.com

Lex Rex - The Law, The King
ISBN: 1-4505-9240-6
A Biblical primer on the purpose, place, and power of civil government. Samuel Rutherford's Lex Rex for the modern reader.

by Thomas Adamo

The ideas in Lex Rex predate modern concepts of nationalism and politics. They are older than the United States Constitution, as well as the American Revolution – where many modern ideas of liberty originated. Lex Rex is even older than the Enlightenment that receives so much credit for concepts such as popular sovereignty, limited government, separation of powers, and individual liberty. Nevertheless, Samuel Rutherford's Lex Rex – written at a time that viewed kings as vessels of divine power – raised a Scriptural standard arguing for the dignity of the people and the accountability of earthly governments. Although some would seek to pigeonhole the book as merely a tract on civil resistance, Lex Rex contains a comprehensive examination of a Christian view of civil government. In doing so, Lex Rex actually formulates a blueprint for freedom applicable for any time and place. Rutherford hoped to demonstrate the need for government based on law instead of the arbitrary decisions of fallible humanity. Throughout this process, the Bible is the final authority and basis for law. This Scriptural base was a primary reason for both the great support and opposition that met Lex Rex.

# # #

Conspiracy Rhetoric
ISBN: 1-4505-7431-9

by Thomas Adamo

Conspiracy Rhetoric seeks to evaluate the growing appeal of conspiracy theories within mainstream American Society. The examination of this phenomenon as a contemporary social narrative proceeds through a content analysis of its public literature in order to determine what common links connect the various expressions of this cultural genre, and how its existence reflects on the larger culture.

# # #

re:Organizing America: We are what we think – both individually, and as a society. Unfortunately, many of the solutions offered to today's problems are mere panaceas that are not the result of serious deliberation. Through a variety of resources, re:Organizing America seeks to engage people in serious thought about the foundations of freedom and American culture. On this basis, it will become evident that an ordered liberty is the true solution to the majority of our contemporary challenges and allow for a dialogue offering real solutions for today's problems. Our editions are lightly edited, but unabridged, in order to make these ideas accessible to the widest possible audience.

The United States of America: State Papers
ISBN: 1-4538-1856-1
The Declaration of Independence, the Articles of Confederation, the Constitution, the Federalist Papers, and Washington's Farewell Address
by re:Organizing America

These essential documents, formulated over the course of twenty years, the Declaration of Independence, the Articles of Confederation, the Constitution, the Federalist Papers, and President Washington's Farewell Address, encapsulate a period of crucial significance to the United States and the world. They are the embodied results of centuries of thought, debate, and experimentation – finally espoused in a practical fashion. The foundations for the experiment of liberty and law that is the United States of America, they are the fundamental guide for securing the blessings of liberty.

# # #

John Locke's Two Essays Concerning Civil Government
ISBN: 1-4538-1859-6

by re:Organizing America

Written in 1689, Locke's Two Treatises of Government disputes the logic of the "divine right of kings," and proceeds to develop a theory of society base on the ideas of natural rights and the social contract. Locke acknowledged the necessity of the state, but saw it primarily as a tool to promote the protection of people and property, as well as the restraint of violence. Based on the consent of the governed, Locke's conception of government highlights the importance of accountability between government and citizen.

# # #

Revolutions: Three Perspectives
ISBN: 1-4538-1860-X
Rousseau's The Social Contract, Paine's Common Sense, and Burke's Reflections on the Revolution in France
by re:Organizing America

Freedom can lead to liberty, or it can descend into chaos. Rousseau's The Social Contract, Paine's Common Sense, and Burke's Reflections on the Revolution in France encompass the ideas, progress, and results of reform and revolutionary change. Rousseau reasoned that people are born free and act as a collective sovereign – owing both freedom and duty under the auspices of the general will, embodied in government. Paine wrote Common Sense in the seminal year of 1775. Using a reasoned and accessible style, he brought forth numerous arguments to demonstrate the logic of launching an American Revolution. Burke's Reflections, while specifically aimed at the French Revolution, demonstrate the superiority of practical solutions over abstract concepts. Each of these works prominently displays the importance of changes leading to freedom. These works demarcate a firm delineation between constructive and destructive change and how it affects human freedom.

# # #

Adam Smith's The Wealth of Nations
ISBN: 1-4538-1862-6

by re:Organizing America

The Wealth of Nations was the world's introduction to capitalism and economics in the modern sense. Smith developed the ideas of free trade and enlightened self interest as in ultimately bringing prosperity and forming a more just society. Freedom, labor, and responsibility form a foundation for the development and accumulation of wealth.

# # #

de Vattel's The Law of Nations
ISBN: 1-4538-1865-0

by re:Organizing America

The Law of Nations focuses on the rights and obligations of what we now term international relations. Outlining ideas that nations should develop reciprocal respect, this work was influential during the founding era of the United States.

# # #

Montesquieu's The Spirit of the Laws
ISBN: 1-4538-1867-7

by re:Organizing America

The result of over twenty years of research The Spirit of the Laws encompasses a vast array of topics and issues. This groundbreaking work provides a comprehensive examination of some of the most important topics relating to liberty. These include constitutionalism, the separation of powers, the primacy of civil liberty and the rule of law, and the power of the local community in establishing political institutions.

# # #

Autobiographies: Benjamin Franklin & Frederick Douglass
ISBN: 1-4538-1869-3

by re:Organizing America

Born over a century apart, one into poverty and the other into slavery, Benjamin Franklin and Frederick Douglass embody the American ideals of success through hard work, vision, and freedom. At the end of their lives, both men were renowned statesmen, admired all over the world. Each is a vivid example of the endless possibilities available to free people.

# # #

Alexis De Tocqueville's Democracy in America
ISBN: 1-4538-1870-7

by re:Organizing America

Summarizing the American experience up to the 1830's Democracy in America explores why the republican government of the United States was succeeding when similar undertakings had failed elsewhere. Based on first hand observations, and balancing the positive and negative attributes of American culture, Alexis de Tocqueville provides a seminal analysis of the economic, political, cultural, and religious components that led to the resounding success of the young United States of America.

# # #

Lewis Carroll's "Alice's Adventures in Wonderland"
ISBN: 1-4515-2383-1
by Family Edition

"Alice was beginning to get very tired of sitting by her sister on the bank, and of having nothing to do: once or twice, she had peeped into the book her sister was reading, but it had no pictures or conversations in it, 'and what is the use of a book,' thought Alice 'without pictures or conversation?'" And so begins, one of the most fantastic adventures of all time... This original text of Alice's Adventures in Wonderland is interspersed with pieces of modern art, creating a fun reading event for the entire family.

# # #

www.ingramcontent.com/pod-product-compliance
Lightning Source LLC
Chambersburg PA
CBHW072137280526
45788CB00002B/671